Essential Lives

Frida Kahlo

Essential Lives

Frida Kahlo

Mexican Artist

by **Emma Carlson Berne**

Content Consultant:
Deborah J. Johnson, PhD
Department of Art and Art History, Providence College

ABDO
Publishing Company

CREDITS

Published by ABDO Publishing Company, 8000 West 78th Street, Edina, Minnesota 55439.

Printed in the United States.

Editors: Patricia Stockland and Mari Kesselring
Copy Editor: Paula Lewis
Interior Design and Production: Nicole Brecke
Cover Design: Nicole Brecke

Library of Congress Cataloging-in-Publication Data
Berne, Emma Carlson.
Frida Kahlo : Mexican artist / by Emma Carlson Berne.
p. cm. — (Essential lives)
Includes bibliographical references and index.
ISBN 978-1-60453-701-7
1. Kahlo, Frida—Juvenile literature. 2. Painters—Mexico—Biography—Juvenile literature. I. Kahlo, Frida. II. Title.

ND259.K33B46 2009
759.972—dc22
[B]

2008055524

Manufactured with paper containing at least 10% post-consumer waste

TABLE OF CONTENTS

Chapter 1

Self Portrait with Velvet Dress

Rising from the Ashes

The busy streets of Mexico City were overcast and chaotic, packed with people, buses, cars, and animals. Vendors hawked fruit and vegetables, businessmen hurried into office buildings, and crowds of laughing children scurried through alleyways. Trolley cars lumbered through the streets. It was September 17, 1925, and 18-year-old Frida Kahlo and her boyfriend, Alejandro Gómez Arias, chose to take a bus home from the market. These new wooden vehicles had recently been introduced to the city, and the drivers were not used to their speed. But Frida and Alejandro were not paying attention to any of that.

They were laughing and talking when Frida realized she was missing her *balero*, a colorful toy parasol she had bought in the market. With her characteristic determination, she insisted that they get off the bus and go back. They could not find the little toy and boarded yet another wooden bus headed back to Coyoacán, the suburb where Frida's parents lived. Frida had no way of knowing that going back to look for the *balero* would change her life forever.

The Accident

Frida and Alejandro took seats in the back of the bus. A few minutes later, a trolley came around the corner and did not stop or even slow down as it approached. As if in slow motion, it pushed the bus against a wall, pressing against it harder and harder. Many years later, Alejandro remembered the bus being squashed so hard that Frida's knees touched the knees of the person across the aisle. Slowly, slowly, the trolley kept squeezing the bus against the wall. The bus bent in the middle more and more. Then, the bus exploded from the pressure, shattering into thousands of pieces and flinging the passengers everywhere. Alejandro was pitched underneath the trolley. Frida was thrown forward, an iron handrail piercing her pelvis like a bayonet.

Screams from wounded passengers echoed through the square. Bodies were scattered like sticks of firewood. Frida's bloody body was placed on a nearby table and, with help, Alejandro pulled the handrail from her body. Years later, Alejandro remembered that Frida's screams were louder than the Red Cross ambulance sirens.

The Dancer

Years later, Alejandro recounted one particular incident during the aftermath of the accident. He remembered that somehow, during the course of the collision, all of Frida's clothes had come off. Someone on the bus had carried a packet of powdered gold. The packet burst when the bus exploded and the powder flew all over Frida's bloody, nude body. When bystanders saw her red figure sprinkled with gold, they cried out "*La bailarina*! [The dancer!]"

No one thought Frida would survive. In the Red Cross hospital, the doctors told her family that her spine was broken in three places. Her collarbone and ribs were broken. Her right foot was crushed, and her right leg had 11 fractures. Her left shoulder had been dislocated, her left arm fractured, and her pelvis broken by the iron handrail.

For a long month, Frida lay in the hospital, encased in a plaster cast and immobile in a box that some said resembled a coffin. This beautiful, athletic, witty girl was now enduring pain more awful than anything she had experienced before. Frida wrote to Alejandro that the therapy for her left arm was the worst, describing the pain and her tears.

Getting Used to Suffering

Life did not improve once Frida was released from the hospital. For two long months, she was confined

Baby Leonardo

At one point, Frida's doctors told her she might never be able to have children because of the damage to her pelvis. Frida drew an elaborate card that mourned the loss of an imaginary child, whom she called Leonardo, and named Alejandro and another school friend as godparents. The card read, "Leonardo was born at the Red Cross in the year of grace, 1925, in the month of September and was baptized in the town of Coyoacán the following year. His mother was Frieda Kahlo, his godparents Isabel Campos and Alejandro Gomez Arias."[1]

to bed in her parents' home while her bones healed. She longed for her friends, for Alejandro, and for the freedom and carelessness of her life before the accident. She was in constant pain. "The only good thing," she wrote to Alejandro on December 5, 1925, "is that I'm starting to get used to suffering."[2]

Finally, in mid-December, Frida was well enough to leave her bed. She could walk, but her pain was no better, especially in her back. One year after the accident, doctors discovered three spine fractures they had missed. Frida was once again confined to her bed and encased in a cast that covered her entire torso. She had no choice but to keep still. She was horribly frustrated. Frida was used to doing: playing pranks with her friends, hopping on and off buses when they were still moving, racing through the city with Alejandro from the library to school

Money and Medical Treatment

Though Frida's family was considered middle class, her parents struggled to pay for their daughter's expensive medical bills. Sometimes Frida would go without X-rays or other examinations because her father could not afford them. In one letter, she tells a friend that she was supposed to have a certain cast put on but it would have to wait because her father did not have the 60 *pesos* needed to pay for it.

to home. She read, she argued, she went to political demonstrations. Now she was confined to bed while her friends were still off doing all of these lovely things.

While Frida's body struggled to repair itself, her mind was leaping about with great energy. She needed something, *anything*, to occupy her time, erase the horrible memories of the accident, and distract herself from the pain. "I was bored as hell . . . so I decided to do something," she wrote years later.[3] That something was art. She asked her photographer

The "Botticelli"

The first picture Frida painted while she was lying in bed was a self-portrait. She could not move around to find a subject, so she had to paint what was in front of her: herself, her family, and her neighborhood friends. Her mother hung a mirror over the bed so Frida could see herself as she painted.

Frida had no formal training in painting, though a printer she worked for had taught her how to draw, and she had engaged in art all her life with her father. Her first painting, *Self-Portrait,* was done in a "naïve" style that was popular during this time. Frida may have worked in this style intentionally to associate herself with this latest modern approach. Frida had studied Italian Renaissance painters as she convalesced and tried to imitate the style of one of the most famous, Sandro Botticelli. She painted herself with pale skin and a long, delicate neck wearing a romantic velvet robe. The colors, though, were dark and gloomy and the figure was stiff.

Frida painted the picture for her boyfriend Alejandro. She was worried he would forget about her as she lay in bed for so many months. After she gave him the painting, she often signed her letters to him, "your Botticeli" [sic].

father for some paints. Her mother ordered a special easel made that could be suspended above the bed so that Frida could paint lying down.

Over the course of her life, Frida wrote reams of letters and diary entries. People know about many of her innermost thoughts and feelings. But she never wrote how it felt to put a brush to canvas for the first time. What emotions filled her mind as she mixed color and spread it glowing onto the blank surface? Did she feel soothed? Excited? She wrote that she started painting out of boredom, not fiery inspiration or an uncontrollable urge. "In this way I began to paint," she wrote dryly many years later.[4] With those seven words, a life of art began. For the rest of Frida's life, painting would sustain her through more suffering and heartbreak than she could imagine.

Tortured by Boredom

For Frida, the inactivity was one of the most difficult parts of her confinement, almost as difficult as the physical pain. On January 10, 1927, she wrote to Alejandro:

"I'm the same as ever—sick—and you can see how boring it is; I don't know what to do any longer. . . .You have to tell me something new, because I was really born to be a flowerpot, never leaving the porch. I'm *buten, buten* bored!!!!!!"[5]

Buten was a word Frida invented; it meant "very, excessively."

A street market in Mexico City around 1920

Chapter 2

Frida Kahlo at four years old

A Childhood of Joy and Pain

Frida Kahlo's Mexico was a place full of bright, vibrant colors. The arid plateau landscape was white adobe, bright sunlight, and yellow sand. Peasant women wore skirts in every color of the rainbow. Bougainvillea blossoms in shocking pink, violet, and coral climbed over walls or spread their blossoms over the sidewalks.

Kahlo became a great artist, and all her life she used the bright colors of her homeland in her paintings. But on July 6, 1907, little Frida did not know anything about colors or light. She was just an hours-old baby, wrapped in soft blankets and cradled in her mother's arms.

Frida's mother, Matilde, did not hold her newest baby for very long. Soon after Frida's birth, Matilde began to feel ill. She hired a wet nurse to take care of the newborn baby and disappeared into her room with the door shut. She would stay there for long periods of time. Matilde may have suffered from depression—no one really knows.

There were plenty of other family members to help with little Frida. Frida's father, Guillermo, had been married once before and had two

Playing with Dates and Names

Frida was born in 1907, but she always said she was born in 1910, the year the Mexican Revolution began. To Frida, 1910 was a far more exciting year in which to be born, so she simply adopted that year. In all her letters and diary entries, Frida shaves three years off her age. Altering reality to make her life different or more interesting was something Frida did her entire life.

When she was an adult, Frida changed her name. Her parents christened her "Frieda," a German name. But when World War II began, Frida did not want to be so closely identified with her German heritage. She dropped the "e" and began spelling her name the way it is known today.

daughters by his first wife. Then he and Matilde married and had four more daughters: Matilde, named after her mother, Adriana, Frida, and the youngest, Cristina.

The family lived in a suburb of Mexico City called Coyoacán. It was a quiet, sleepy little place with comfortable houses, fields of crops, and plenty of stray dogs panting in the dust in the village square. When Guillermo had looked for a place to build a house, he had wanted to live in a suburb that was even quieter and farther from the city, but his wife convinced him that Coyoacán was far enough.

He agreed, and in 1904 Guillermo built a traditional Mexican house for his growing family. It was a spacious home with the rooms arranged around a patio and a beautiful tropical garden. Guillermo set up a photography studio. Soon, he was making a good living taking architectural photographs on commission.

Frida's Family

Frida's father had not always been called Guillermo, and he was not Mexican. Frida claimed her father was born to Jewish parents in the town of Baden-Baden, Germany, in 1872.

The Kahlo family including Frida, center

His parents named him Wilhelm. Jakob, his father, was a successful jeweler who also sold photography equipment. The family had plenty of money—enough to send Wilhelm to university. When he was 19, though, Wilhelm's life changed.

He regularly suffered from seizures. Wilhelm always told his family that he fell while he was at the university and that the seizures started soon afterward. But some scholars believe Wilhelm had epilepsy long before he was 19. He might have told this story because he was ashamed of his condition.

Wilhelm also might have received brain injuries in the fall. These injuries, combined with the seizures, made it difficult for him to concentrate while studying. Around the same time, Wilhelm's mother, Henriette, died and his father quickly remarried. Wilhelm did not care for his new stepmother and wanted to get away.

In 1891, Jakob gave Wilhelm enough money for boat passage to Mexico. When Wilhelm set foot on Mexican soil, he changed his name to Guillermo. From that moment on, he considered himself a Mexican and never returned to Germany.

Guillermo Kahlo worked at odd jobs and married a Mexican woman. She died giving birth to their second daughter in 1898. Then, Guillermo met a beautiful young woman named Matilde Calderón. She was tiny, with

Guillermo and Matilde

Guillermo and Matilde, Frida's parents, met in an unusual way. When Guillermo's first wife was dying during the birth of their second daughter, the distraught husband called Isabel Calderón, Matilde's mother, for help. Isabel came to assist and she brought her daughter with her. That night, according to Frida, Guillermo fell in love with Matilde.

big, dark eyes and long, black hair. One day, she would become Frida's mother.

Matilde was born in the city of Oaxaca. Like her new husband, she also had an exotic heritage. Her father was a native Indian, and her mother was the daughter of a Spanish general. She did not, however, have very much education and was mostly illiterate. Frida remembers that her mother was "like a little bell from Oaxaca. When she went to market, she gracefully cinched her waist and carried her basket coquettishly."[1]

Wild from the Start

From the beginning, Frida was always different from her calm older sisters. She was independent and creative even as a little girl. As soon as she could walk, Frida started creating mischief too—a trait that would continue for the rest of her life.

Frida and her little sister Cristina used to climb out the window during their catechism classes and run off to a nearby orchard. They would sit in the trees and pluck fruit from the branches. At dinner, when their devoutly Catholic mother would pray before the meal, the two would kick each other to keep from laughing.

When Frida was little, her family had a comfortable life, with enough money for whatever they needed. Guillermo had a good job as the official government photographer of Mexico's Colonial and pre-Columbian architecture. This was under the Mexican dictator Porfirio Díaz. When Díaz fell from power in 1911, however, Guillermo lost his job—and a large source of his income. The Kahlos scraped by for many years. They even had to mortgage their house.

These financial difficulties were hard on Guillermo. He was constantly grumpy and depressed. He spent long hours at his studio in the city away from his family. When he was home, he would

The Story of Matilde

Frida's mother was a very strict Catholic. She and Frida's father could be cold and rigid with their children. Sometimes this created unhappiness in the household. Frida once told this story about her older sister, Matilde:

"At seven I helped my 15-year-old sister Matilde escape to Veracruz with her boyfriend. . . . When Maty went away, my father didn't say a word. . . . We spent four years without seeing [Matilde], and while we were in a street car one day my father said to me: 'We'll never find her.' I consoled him and my hopes were really sincere. I was 12 years old when a friend . . . told me: 'On the street where the doctors live there's a woman who looks exactly like you and her name is Matilde Kahlo.' At the back of the patio, in the fourth room off a wide hallway, I found her. The room was filled with light and birds and Matilde was bathing herself with a hose. . . . The first thing I did was tell my father I'd found her. I visited her several times, and tried to convince my mother to see her, but she refused."[2]

shut himself in his private parlor, where he would read and play the piano.

There was only one person in the house Guillermo liked to be with: his daughter Frida. She was his favorite, he always said, because she was smart and, of all his daughters, the most like him. Guillermo still suffered from seizures, and Frida would help him. If they were out when he fell, she would watch to make sure no one stole his camera.

In addition to his photography business, Guillermo liked to paint in the parks on the weekends. Frida would go with him when he painted. He taught her to take photographs and encouraged her to examine the things she found along the way: shells, insects, bones, and feathers. As an adult, Kahlo often said that these weekends with her father were some of the happiest of her childhood.

A Serious Illness

Frida was six years old in 1913. She was a healthy, strong, cheerful child who only knew the love of her family and the security of their house in Coyoacán. This changed in 1914 when Frida contracted polio. There was no cure for the disease and many people, especially children, died from it. Frida had to

Understanding Polio

Polio is a virus that begins with headaches, muscle aches, and fever. If not treated, a person can become partially or completely paralyzed or suffer muscle damage. During Frida's childhood, there was no cure. But in 1952, Jonas Salk developed a vaccine. Today, polio is rare in developed countries because children are immunized.

remain in bed for nine months while her mother and sisters nursed her. Frida remembered having her right leg, which was afflicted with the disease, bathed with hot towels and water with crushed walnuts.

When Frida recovered, she had changed. Her right leg was smaller and thinner than her left and would remain so for the rest of her life. Frida was extremely self-conscious about her leg. When she was photographed, even as a teenager, she would hide her right leg behind her left. She limped when she walked and had to wear special little boots to support her ankles.

Frida's father insisted that she start playing sports in order to strengthen her disease-weakened body. At that time, it was very unusual for a well-bred Mexican girl to play soccer, box, and wrestle, but Frida loved it all. Slowly, with time and lots of exercise, Frida regained the strength she had lost and became a strong, spunky girl once more.

A photograph taken by Guillermo Kahlo

Chapter 3

Frida's mother was a devout Catholic.

Adventures at School

When Frida was 15, her parents began looking for a high school for her to attend. Guillermo, who was an atheist, did not want his daughter attending a Catholic high school. Most likely against the wishes of his devoutly Catholic wife,

Guillermo enrolled his favorite daughter in the National Preparatory School. This was the best high school in Mexico and was in Mexico City, about an hour's trolley ride from the family's house.

Frida was ready to go. Like many teenagers, she often complained that Coyoacán was dull and too quiet. She was ready for some adventure. Located in the heart of the city, *La Preparatoria*, as it was called in Spanish, was the perfect place for a bold teenage girl bursting with creativity.

The school was a raucous, energetic place. The finest students in Mexico City attended classes there. They frequently organized and participated in political demonstrations, rallies, and vigorous intellectual debates. This energy frequently overflowed into pranks too.

Frida was in her element. At last, she found a place where she could express the ebullient, bawdy personality she was rapidly developing. Frida was very smart but not terribly interested in going to

One of a Few Girls

At the time of Frida's entrance into La Preparatoria, girls had only recently been permitted to enroll. Frida was one of only 35 girls out of a total student body of 2,000. When she first entered high school, Frida thought she might want to study to become a doctor.

Frida at 18 years old

class all the time. Mostly, she liked to spend time with her friends, a group of students who called themselves the Cachuchas, which was the name for the caps they all wore. The Cachuchas were the smartest—and craziest—students in school. They were known for their constant reading, ongoing political arguments, and elaborate pranks. Once, they tossed a huge firecracker outside a classroom where a famous professor was lecturing. Another time, they rode a donkey through the crowded hallways of the school. When they were not causing trouble, the Cachuchas liked to go to the Ibero American Library, a beautiful old library in town. They would hide in little, cozy alcoves and read philosophy and history.

The Wild Child

Frida emerged as one of the leaders of this group. People were drawn to her clever, frequently vulgar sense of humor. She said whatever was on her mind, without worrying about what people would think. She often purposely flaunted convention. For a family photograph taken by her father, Frida stood with her sisters. All the young women wore fluffy, pale cotton dresses and pearl jewelry. Their hair was wavy and bobbed in the style of the time. Teenage Frida, who stood in the middle, wore a

Learning to Draw

Frida had no formal art training, but she did have innate talent and guidance. Early in her life, she worked for a printer named Fernando Fernández. She needed an after-school job to help support her family. Fernández hired Frida as an engraver but noticed that she had a special eye for form and style. He taught her to draw and encouraged her to think about pursuing art seriously.

perfectly fitted man's three-piece suit, complete with tie, cane, and flower in the buttonhole. Her dark hair was parted severely in the middle and tied tightly back. She even stood like a man, with one hand in her pants pocket and one on her cane.

Frida's eyebrows became a symbol to her, and to others, of her unusual personality. Frida was very beautiful, with a delicate figure, shiny hair, and a full mouth. But her eyebrows were so thick and heavy that they met in the middle. Many women would have plucked them, but Frida refused to pluck. She considered her brows a trademark and even penciled them in darker and heavier.

Frida did not spend all of her time reading and playing jokes. She also fell in love soon after arriving at La Preparatoria. Her boyfriend was Alejandro Gómez Arias, the unofficial leader of the Cachuchas. Alejandro was known to

A Poem by Frida

Frida was intensely creative and often wrote her thoughts in letters and poems. In this excerpt from a 1922 prose poem, she talks about a man she imagines following her through a town at night:

"All I had done was smile, but there was innocence in me and in the depth of my silence.

He, he was following me. Like my shadow, irreproachable and unsteady.

At night he sobbed a song . . ."[1]

be handsome, smart, charismatic, and an excellent speaker. But the two teenagers had to sneak around to see each other; Frida's parents did not approve of her having a boyfriend.

Frida was quite passionate about her love for Alejandro. She wrote him scores of letters that reveal her impetuous, unbridled nature. In one letter, dated August 18, 1924, Frida writes,

> *See you tomorrow, let's have a good night and think that big buddies have to love each other very, very, very, very, very, very, very, very much . . . with M as in music or mundo [world].*
>
> *First premise: Big buddies should love each other very much*
>
> *Second premise: Alex and Friducha [a pet name] are big buddies*
>
> *Conclusion: Therefore, Alex and Friducha should love each other very much.* [2]

Meeting Diego

Alejandro was Frida's love, but she was also interested in another man at La Preparatoria. This person was not a student, though. Diego Rivera, a famous artist, had been commissioned to paint a mural in the auditorium of the school. Rivera was one of the best-known artists in Mexico.

It is not surprising that Frida was interested in Rivera. A very unusual-looking man, Rivera was very tall and very fat, with a big potbelly. He had bug eyes like a frog and dark hair that he wore combed back from his forehead. Everyone who knew him agreed that Diego was spectacularly ugly—so ugly, in fact, that he was almost handsome. Women found Diego very attractive. He frequently brought his beautiful young girlfriend and future wife, Lupe Marín, with him while he painted.

Diego took his work very seriously. Every day, he stood on the network of elaborate scaffolding erected around the walls of the auditorium and intensely worked on his murals. Frida was fascinated by him. She would hide in the shadows to watch him work. She would play pranks on him

Panzón

Frida and her friends were not very nice to Diego Rivera when he was painting at La Preparatoria. Their favorite nickname for him was panzón—fat belly. They also thought he looked dirty, which may have been true—Diego was famous for hating baths. But Frida would always defend Diego, saying that if she married him, she would bathe and clean him.

too, like stealing his lunch when he left the room. Once, she soaped the stairs near the auditorium, hoping to make him slip.

Later in his life, Diego described his memory of the first time he met Frida. He said that he was painting one day on the scaffolding, accompanied by Lupe Marín. He heard a ruckus outside the auditorium doors, which then flew open, and a young girl was pushed inside. Diego said that he noticed this girl's unusual beauty and dignity immediately. The girl asked if she could sit and watch the artist work. When he agreed, she took a seat and

Diego Rivera

By the time Frida met Diego Rivera in 1922, he had spent almost his entire life immersed in art. He was born in Mexico in 1886. Both of his parents were teachers and sent him to school at an early age. A brilliant student, Diego learned to read when he was only four. His parents soon realized he had a talent for art and sent him to art classes at an academy in Mexico City when he was ten. By the time he was 12, Diego was completely devoted to painting.

When he was 20, the governor of the Mexican state of Veracruz awarded Rivera a scholarship to study art in Europe. A year after receiving the scholarship, the young painter traveled through Spain, France, Belgium, and Holland and met many famous artists who nurtured his talent: Chaim Soutine, Amedeo Modigliani, and Pablo Picasso.

Rivera remained in Europe for 15 years, until 1921. Upon his return to Mexico, his public art became very important to post-Revolutionary Mexico. Rivera expressed ideas in his murals that not only captured Mexican history and social commentary but also conveyed his political beliefs.

sat like a stone for three hours, her eyes fixed on his paintbrush. Eventually, Lupe grew jealous of the girl and began berating her. But Frida just stared at the older woman. She was not afraid of anything in life she had encountered so far. She even boasted to her friends that one day, she would bear Diego's child—even though she was 15 and he was 36. She had no idea that one day this man would be her husband.

Diego Rivera

Chapter 4

As she grew up, Frida became a deep thinker.

Darkness and Light

Diego Rivera soon finished his murals in La Preparatoria auditorium and moved on to other work. Frida may have tucked the memory of him in a corner of her mind or forgot about him entirely. Three years after Rivera left, Frida had other, much bigger problems to worry about.

The horrible, nightmarish accident changed Frida's life forever. Though she had suffered pain from polio when she was six, the memory of that illness had faded. Frida had spent years climbing trees, wrestling the neighborhood boys, and racing up and down the Mexico City streets with the Cachuchas.

Now, in 1925, Frida was living in a different world—one that her friends did not understand. Hers was a life of doctors, nurses, X-rays, and long, long hours flat on her back in bed, encased in plaster casts. But the change was more than just physical. Frida felt that she had aged overnight with her newfound knowledge of suffering. In September 1926, one year after her accident, Frida wrote to Alejandro,

> *Why do you study so much? What secret are you looking for? . . . I already know everything, without reading or writing. A short while ago . . . I was a girl walking in a world of colors,*

Manipulating Suffering

Kahlo suffered a great deal of genuine pain throughout her life, beginning with her bus accident. She was hospitalized multiple times and eventually underwent 30 surgeries. Frida's letters to Alejandro in the months after her accident reflect the pain she lived in. However, biographer Hayden Herrera has speculated that Kahlo also used her suffering to bind others to her. At one point, she tells Alejandro in a letter that she wishes she could describe to him every moment of her suffering. Later, Herrera states, she would use her pain to keep Rivera near her.

of clear and tangible shapes. . . . Now I live in a painful planet, transparent as ice. It's as if I had learned everything at the same time, in a matter of seconds. . . . I grew up in a few instants and now everything is dull and flat.[1]

Frida insisted on describing all of her pain to Alejandro. An April 1927 letter read,

They fitted me for the plaster cast on Friday, and since then I've been suffering sheer martyrdom; I'm suffocating, my lungs and my whole back are in agony, I can't move my leg and I can hardly walk any more and sleep even less. Can you imagine that they hung me up by my head and afterwards I had to stand for over an hour on tiptoe while I was being dried with hot air. . . . I'll have to stand this torture for three or four months and if it doesn't help, I really do want to die, for I can't take it anymore.[2]

His girlfriend's suffering may have been too much for Alejandro to handle. They were both only teenagers. But Frida's dependence on

Letter to Europe

In this excerpt from a 1927 letter to Alejandro during his European trip, Frida's loneliness and longing are obvious:

"Even though they take me out into the sunlight . . . every morning, I don't feel I have gotten any better, since the pains are always the same and I am very thin. But in spite of this, I want to have faith, as I told you in the other letter. . . . You can't imagine with what pleasure I would give all my life just to kiss you. I think this time I have really suffered, I must deserve it, right?"[3]

Alejandro's love only increased during the months she spent in bed. She begged him to come and visit her every day, but as the weeks passed, he came less and less.

In 1927, Alejandro went on an extended trip to Europe. No one knows if his family sent him away to get some distance from Frida, or if he wanted to go himself. Either way, by the time he returned several months later, he had made up his mind. The two had drifted apart.

All during the long months in bed, in between the letters, Frida was painting. She

Communism

Communism is a political and social philosophy that promotes the idea of a society without social classes, rich people or poor people, or private ownership of property. In an ideal communist land, everything would be owned by all the people equally, and everyone would be treated the same, without rank or discrimination. The opposite of communism is capitalism, in which people strive to earn money or accomplishments in an effort to advance their place in society. The best-known communist country was the former Soviet Union. Modern-day China is an example of a communist country still in existence.

Many intellectuals, artists, and writers during Kahlo's time, including Kahlo herself, believed that communism could help Mexico. Many of the peasants were poor, they argued, while other people were very rich. They believed Mexican society should be more equal. The Russian Revolution inspired these Mexican leftists. After the Mexican Revolution, they hoped communism would create a classless society in Mexico where everyone would be treated equally, including peasants and indigenous peoples.

Alejandro Gómez Arias

Alejandro Gómez Arias was an important person in Frida's life. They remained close until Frida's death. Alejandro grew up to become a respected professional in Mexico. He led student protests against the oppressive Mexican government while he was in college at the University of Mexico and also founded a radio station at the school. Alejandro eventually became a well-known lawyer and political journalist.

painted herself, her sisters, her friends, all things she could see while lying in bed with her special easel. By the time Frida was allowed to get up and rejoin the world, she had decided not to return to La Preparatoria for school. She was going to be an artist instead.

Becoming an Artist

Kahlo was ready for a new life. She was not the same girl who had laughed with Alejandro on the bus just a few years earlier. She had a new occupation and needed some new friends to go with it. Germán de Campo, a schoolmate, began taking Kahlo around to parties and gatherings full of left-wing intellectuals. She liked the creative, energetic people she met at these parties, and they liked her. Though still recovering from her injuries, Kahlo was bold, unconventional, and never afraid to speak her mind.

Some of the people Kahlo met were members of the Mexican Communist Party, as were many Mexican intellectuals and artists in the late 1920s.

Frida and Diego at a communist rally

The more she heard about the ideals and positions of communism, the more she was drawn to it: rejecting elitism and wealth, opposing capitalism, and appreciating the peasants and workers of Mexico. In 1928, Kahlo officially joined the Mexican Communist Party.

Kahlo learned that Diego Rivera was painting murals at the Ministry of Education. Rivera had recently divorced Lupe Marín. He had become fatter and more famous than before. He was a dedicated communist and an unofficial leader of the Mexican Communist Party. Kahlo was still fascinated by Rivera, especially since she was an artist now too. She was determined to talk to him. So one day she packed three of her paintings and went to see him. Straight out, she asked Rivera if he thought she was any good as an artist. "I was immediately impressed," Rivera later wrote. "The canvases revealed an unusual energy of expression, precise delineation of character, and true severity."[4]

The next week, Rivera visited the Kahlo's home to view more of her work. Years later, he remembered that Kahlo was wearing overalls and that she danced him through the house, which was full of light, to the room where she painted. Rivera was captivated by this small, slender, dark-haired woman with the heavy eyebrows and unvarnished personality. And she was equally captivated by the huge, frog-eyed, fat man who painted such intense murals.

In the late 1920s, Frida had mostly recovered from the bus accident. She decided to become an artist.

Chapter 5

Frida Kahlo and Diego Rivera

Frida and Diego

Over the next weeks and months, Kahlo fell in love with Rivera, even though she was only 22 and he was 42. Art played a central role in their courtship. Rivera painted an image of Kahlo into one of his murals in the Mexican

Ministry of Education building. The two critiqued each other's paintings. Rivera would ask Kahlo's advice on color and form when he painted, and he usually listened to what she had to say. He considered Kahlo an immensely talented artist. For her part, Kahlo once told a reporter, "Diego showed me the revolutionary sense of life and the true sense of color."[1]

Rivera and Kahlo were married on August 21, 1929. When Rivera asked Kahlo's father for permission to marry her, Guillermo warned him that she was a devil. What is more, he told the famous artist, "Notice that my daughter is a sick person and all her life she will be sick; she is intelligent, but not pretty. Think it over if you want, and if you wish to get married, I give you my permission."[2] Rivera did not care. In each other, he and Kahlo had found equal passion, vibrancy, and creativity.

Diego on Frida

Rivera's genuine admiration for his wife is clear in this excerpt from an interview with Mexican art critic Raquel Tibol:

"Frida Kahlo is really a marvelous human being with a vital force and an ability to stand pain far beyond the normal. As is natural, a higher sensitivity, incredibly pure and susceptible, is united to this power. . . . Although her paintings do not extend over the large areas of our murals, by their content in intensity and depth, more [than] equal to our quantity and quality, Frida Kahlo is the greatest of Mexican painters . . ."[3]

The wedding was as unconventional as they were. Rivera and Kahlo were married at the Coyoacán town hall in a small, simple ceremony, with no guests and only two witnesses. Kahlo wore a traditional Mexican skirt and blouse she had borrowed from her maid. She was still wearing a brace on her damaged right foot and was pleased at the way the long, gathered skirt hid the apparatus.

The reception was a harbinger of Kahlo and Rivera's turbulent marriage. The raucous party was held at a friend's house. Everyone was roaringly drunk. At one point, Rivera's first wife, Lupe Marín, stormed into the room, grabbed Kahlo's skirt and yanked it up high, exposing her legs still withered from the accident and the polio. Lupe then turned to the silent, staring wedding guests and shouted, "Do you see those two canes? That's what Diego's going to have to put up with now and he used to have my legs!"[4] Then she left the room.

Later in the party, Rivera got very drunk, and according to Kahlo, started shooting things with his pistol. He broke a man's finger and

Frida on Diego

Kahlo loved her husband very much, but he also caused her a great deal of pain throughout her life. She once said of her husband, "I suffered two grave accidents in my life. One in which a streetcar knocked me down. The other accident is Diego."[5]

Frida often wore flamboyant hairstyles after her marriage.

Kahlo went home crying. Rivera followed after her the next morning.

A Young Wife

Kahlo did not paint much in the months following her marriage. Taking care of her husband took most of her time. She had to quickly learn how to be a wife to the work-obsessed, brilliant, self-absorbed Rivera. She had help from Lupe Marín, who, despite her outburst at the wedding, soon became a good friend to Kahlo. Marín started visiting Kahlo during the days when Rivera was gone and taught her to cook his favorite foods. She also told Kahlo to visit Rivera on his scaffolding every noontime and bring him his lunch in a basket.

Kahlo loved caring for her husband—and he loved accepting her ministrations in return. He would often work on his murals until he collapsed from exhaustion. Then Kahlo would patiently nurse him back to health.

Kahlo also began dressing differently after her wedding. Previously, she dressed in the simple, work-oriented garments that many young communists wore: overalls, denim jackets, and plain canvas pants. She tied her long black hair back in a severe bun. But Rivera loved the texture and color of traditional Mexican dress. So Kahlo began wearing long, ruffled skirts, full

The Independent Woman

Much of what Kahlo did in the early years of her marriage was aimed at pleasing her husband. She took care of Rivera in typical housewifely ways, such as cooking and decorating their house. Although he liked to be waited on, Rivera also liked women who were independent and strong. He expected Kahlo to say what she was thinking, to have her own friends, and to go places alone.

cotton blouses, and embroidered shawls. She braided and arranged her hair in elaborate styles woven with fresh flowers and adorned herself with long, heavy earrings, stacks of bracelets, and strings of beads around her neck. Educated Mexico City women such as Kahlo usually wore simple silk or cotton dresses in the "flapper" style of the 1920s and had short hair pressed into permanent waves. But Kahlo loved her clothes. The bright colors and beautiful fabrics pleased her keen artistic

The People of Tehuantepec

Kahlo's style of dress was unique, but it was not entirely her own. Her long, ruffled skirts, layers of petticoats, embroidered blouses, and flower headdresses were drawn from the clothing of the women from the Isthmus of Tehuantepec. The region is south of Mexico City, near Oaxaca. The land narrows like a waist, making Tehuantepec the place with the shortest distance between the Gulf of Mexico and the Pacific Ocean.

The people of Tehuantepec belong to an indigenous group called Zapotecs. The women are referred to as Tehuanas, and they are considered very beautiful, elegant, strong, and brave. Even more remarkable, the women conduct most of the business in the region, rather than the men, as is the norm in the rest of Mexico.

Like Kahlo, who had visited the area several times, many people admired the Tehuana dress. Women usually wore decorated cotton blouses and purple or red velvet skirts. On special occasions, women wore a headdress called a *resplandor* that encircled the head with stiff, starched lace standing out in ruffles, making the woman's face look like the center of a flower surrounded by petals. While many patriotic Mexican women adopted this native costume to show their nationalism on holidays and for other festivities, Kahlo embraced it as her everyday clothing.

senses. Every day, she would take her time trying on different outfits, choosing jewelry, fixing her hair, and putting on makeup. Many historians have pointed out that Frida treated her appearance as a work of art—something beautiful that she was carefully creating.

In Cuernavaca

In October 1929, the couple suffered the first crisis of their marriage. Rivera was expelled from the Communist Party, even though he had been a devout member and local leader for years. Party officials were upset that Rivera continued to take mural commissions from the Mexican government, which suppressed the Mexican Communist Party. The Communist Party officially opposed the reigning Mexican government, so they considered Rivera's actions a betrayal. He was devastated. The party was like a family to him. In solidarity, Kahlo resigned her own membership, though she was also a devout and active communist.

After the expulsion, Rivera and Kahlo felt like they needed to get out of Mexico City for a while and let angry tempers subside. In December 1929, Rivera accepted a mural commission in Cuernavaca, about

50 miles (80 km) from Mexico City. The lovely little town was also the perfect place for the two to enjoy a delayed honeymoon.

For Kahlo, the first few months in Cuernavaca were full of delicious food, lots of sleep, and pleasant excursions around the Mexican countryside. She was excited, no doubt, because of another special event in her life: she was in the first trimester of pregnancy. But after three months, the doctors told her the baby was in the wrong position. Frida had an abortion. Moreover, the doctors explained that she might never be able to bear a child because of the damage done to her spine and pelvis during the bus accident.

Kahlo was depressed by this news, and the behavior of her husband did not improve her condition. Soon after their marriage, Rivera resumed the promiscuous life he was accustomed to before his wedding.

The Elephant and the Dove

Guillermo Kahlo, Frida's father, called the pair "the elephant and the dove," referring to their opposite physical appearances. The difference between the two is especially striking in their wedding photograph. The tiny, slender Kahlo, who weighed less than 100 pounds (45 kg), sits primly on a chair, her legs crossed. Her neat, delicate features and smoothed-back hair contrast sharply with the six-foot, 250-pound (113-kg) Rivera, who stands next to her. His clothes are wrinkled and pulled over his massive belly, and his bulging eyes and thick lips stand out below a shock of messy dark hair.

He constantly had affairs with other women, often the assistants and models he hired to help him with his murals. Kahlo stormed at Rivera and cried when she learned of his infidelity, but he insisted that she was his soul mate and the other women meant nothing. As always, the couple remained unique. Kahlo would often befriend Rivera's other lovers. Kahlo also had affairs of her own during the marriage. And in some cases, Rivera's lovers would become her lovers.

Theirs was a dramatic marriage of extremes. Kahlo and Rivera had huge arguments, complete with throwing china and screaming. But, their many friends observed, they were also passionately in love and addressed each other constantly in tender endearments. They often stood together on the scaffolding where Rivera worked and embraced and kissed for a long time.

Kahlo completed this painting, titled Frieda and Diego Rivera *in 1931.*

Chapter 6

Kahlo and Rivera visited the United States.

In the United States

In November 1930, Kahlo and Rivera were offered the opportunity to have a great adventure. Diego's fame had spread to the United States, and he received a commission to paint one of his famous murals on the walls of the Luncheon

Club of the San Francisco Stock Exchange. The United States was experiencing an economic depression. U.S. patrons hoped the cultural unity and patriotic spirit that muralists such as Rivera, Orozco, and Siqueiros had inspired in Mexico would also inspire U.S. citizens. Kahlo had never been outside of Mexico before. Now, not only was she going to the United States, but she was also going as the wife of an internationally famous artist.

They were treated as celebrities upon their arrival. The press met them everywhere they went, requesting interviews and photographs. For the most part though, the press reports from the time focused on Rivera. He was the famous artist, after all. Unlike her husband, Kahlo had not yet learned how to cultivate her flamboyant personality and appearance into a celebrity image. To the reporters, she was merely Mrs. Rivera, Diego's beautiful, young wife.

Kahlo and Rivera settled into their quarters in San Francisco, and Rivera went to work on his mural, resuming his usual nonstop work schedule. Meanwhile, Kahlo explored the city. She was quite an unusual figure on the streets of the cosmopolitan city, with her long, colorful Mexican skirts and heavy stone necklaces. She fascinated Rivera's American friends. Kahlo, on the other hand, did not think very much of the Americans. She wrote to a friend in Mexico that they had "faces like unbaked rolls (especially the old women)."[1] She did make one good friend though: Dr. Leo Eloesser, a physician who gave her advice about her continuing problems with her right foot. Dr. Eloesser also examined Kahlo and told her that some of her pain was caused by a crooked spine, a condition also called scoliosis.

For all her dislike of American looks, Kahlo enjoyed trying out typical American activities. With Rivera's friends or assistants, Kahlo ate out and went shopping. Kahlo did not spend all her time playing in San Francisco. She also worked.

Dr. Leo Eloesser

When Kahlo and Rivera arrived in California, they quickly made friends with Leo Eloesser, who was a doctor at San Francisco General Hospital. He was especially close to Kahlo and would remain her personal physician for the rest of her life.

Eloesser was an excellent thoracic and bone surgeon. He often went on humanitarian missions to various countries and served the poor in remote Mexican villages. But he was also a musician and often held chamber music gatherings at his apartment. While friends such as the famous violinist Isaac Stern played their instruments, Eloesser would play his viola.

Eloesser could be just as unconventional as his most famous patient. Kahlo biographer Hayden Herrera writes that Eloesser also had an unusual habit of taking his sailboat out in the middle of the night. He would sail out to a little island off of San Francisco Bay, spend the night on the water, and then sail back to the city in time for work the next morning.

In 1931, she painted a wedding portrait of herself and Rivera and painted a portrait of Leo Eloesser as a gift to him. Also in 1931, Kahlo produced what many critics consider her first important work—a portrait of friend and horticulturalist Luther Burbank. Titled *Luther Burbank*, the painting was different from all of her previous work. It depicted Burbank standing in a desolate landscape. He holds the leaves and stem of a plant in his hands. What is remarkable about the painting is that the lower half of Burbank's body is replaced with a tree trunk and roots. This was the first time that Kahlo had painted from her imagination rather than interpreting what was right in front of her. Fantasy and imagination would become essential to Kahlo's art in the future.

Across the Continent

Rivera finished his work on the stock exchange murals. After a return trip to Mexico, the couple moved in November 1931 to New York City, where Rivera was to have a retrospective at the Museum of Modern Art. Just as in San Francisco, the pair was honored everywhere they went. They met many famous people, including Nelson Rockefeller, who became a close friend.

Kahlo loved the vibrancy and excitement of New York. She became more relaxed and, as a result, more flamboyant. She would often do or say outrageous things in front of other people just to see their reactions.

Rivera's exhibition was very well received, and in the spring of 1932, he accepted a commission to paint a mural at the Detroit Institute of Arts. He loved the mechanics and industry of Detroit, but Kahlo was not very impressed. She thought Detroit was ugly and old after the brilliancy of New York. She amused herself by behaving even more outrageously.

One famous anecdote about Kahlo and her outlandish sense of humor concerns the couple's friendship with Henry Ford. Ford was the founder of Ford Motor Company and Detroit's most wealthy and famous resident. He was also known to be anti-Semitic and Kahlo found

Under Her Skirts

Kahlo enjoyed playing with controversy. She would often wear ruffled white petticoats under her long skirts, in keeping with traditional Mexican style. The only difference was that she would embroider vulgar Mexican sayings on the hems of her petticoats so that the words would flash when she moved.

this out. She and Rivera disliked prejudice of any kind. So, one night at a dinner party, she turned to Henry Ford, who was sitting next to her, and asked innocently, in front of the entire group, "Mr. Ford, are you Jewish?"[2] There is no record of Henry Ford's response, but apparently he was not too angry; at another party later, he asked Kahlo to dance several times.

Inspiration from Heartbreak

In July 1932, Kahlo suffered what was the most traumatic incident of her life since her bus accident. Soon after her arrival in Detroit, she discovered she was pregnant again. After much deliberation with her doctors, she decided to keep the baby, despite the warnings that she might not be able to carry the child to term.

But on July 4, Kahlo began bleeding and was rushed to Henry

Jewish Heritage

Both Kahlo and Rivera claimed Jewish heritage, of which they were very proud. Kahlo claimed her father was Jewish. Guillermo's parents were both Hungarian Jews who had emigrated from Hungary to Germany when they were young. Rivera's family had descended from *conversos*—Jews who had been forced to convert to Catholicism during the Spanish Inquisition. Once, when Kahlo and Rivera stayed in Detroit, they learned that their hotel did not admit Jews. The famous couple loudly announced that, in that case, they would have to leave. Eager to avoid a fuss, the hotel hastily rescinded its policy.

Kahlo longed to have a child but was never able to carry a pregnancy to term.

Ford Hospital in Detroit. After four months of pregnancy, she had a miscarriage.

Kahlo was devastated and deeply mourned the child she had been unable to bear. In the depth of her grief, she painted one of her most powerful paintings. *Henry Ford Hospital* shows Kahlo on a hospital bed, naked and bleeding, against the background of Detroit's industry. Various symbolic objects are painted floating above and below her body, attached like balloons to her figure.

But the difficult times were not over for Kahlo. In September, she received a telegram saying that her mother was dying. She traveled to Mexico City and arrived just before Matilde died of cancer on September 15.

Once again, Kahlo expressed her grief in her work. Upon her return to Detroit, she painted another powerful piece, *My Birth*. The painting depicts a woman whose face and torso are covered by a white sheet, indicating that she is dead, giving birth to Kahlo's own head, adult-sized and apparently dead also. Art critics have speculated that this painting is an amalgam of Kahlo's thoughts on birth and death and combines her mother's death, her baby's death and lost life, and her own birth.

Kahlo was glad to leave Detroit in March 1933 to return to New York and her friends there. Rivera had received a commission to paint a mural in Rockefeller Center. He began as usual, but with his typical love of controversy, he painted the head of Russian communist leader Vladimir Lenin on the body of a labor leader in the mural. The capitalist Rockefellers were outraged at this trick and dismissed him from the project with the balance of the money owed him. The couple left the United States in December.

In the News

Rivera was the true celebrity during the couple's U.S. travels. This excerpt from a *New York Times* article on Rivera's arrival in New York does not even mention Kahlo:

"Diego Rivera, one of the world's leading artists, arrived in New York Friday from his native Mexico to prepare for the exhibition of his work which the Museum of Modern Art will hold in its galleries at 730 Fifth Avenue next month. The honor of a one-man show has been accorded by the museum to only one other living artist, Henri Matisse . . . "[3]

A screen covered the offending part of Rivera's mural at the Rockefeller Center in New York.

Chapter 7

Kahlo and Rivera moved into a new house designed by fellow Mexican artist Juan O'Gorman in San Angel.

Other Lovers

Kahlo and Rivera returned to Mexico in December 1933. Rivera had arranged for a new house to be built in a neighborhood of Mexico City called San Angel. The house was modern, made of two cubes linked by a walkway. One was Rivera's cube, painted pink, and one was Kahlo's, painted blue. The couple would occupy the San Angel home on and off for the rest of their lives. Their friends sometimes commented that the house was symbolic of Kahlo's and Rivera's relationship: each cube distinct and separate, yet permanently linked.

Despite the new house, the period following the return to Mexico was stormy and tempestuous. Rivera was furious at losing the Rockefeller Center commission and unhappy about coming back to Mexico. He had wanted to remain in New York and blamed Kahlo for insisting that they return. Selfishly, Rivera sought to hurt Kahlo by starting an affair with her sister Cristina.

When Kahlo found out, she was devastated. She was very close to Cristina and could not dismiss this affair as she had the others. Kahlo moved out of the San Angel house

Letter to Diego

Despite his cruelty, Kahlo loved Rivera passionately, as she wrote in this letter:

"Diego: Nothing compares to your hands nothing like the green-gold of your eyes. My body is filled with you for days and days. you are the mirror of the night. the violent flash of lightning. the dampness of the earth. The hollow of your armpits is my shelter. my fingertips touch your blood. All my joy is to feel life spring from your flower-fountain that mine keeps to fill all the paths of my nerves which are yours."[1]

and took up residence in a rented apartment in the city center. She cut off the long, luxurious black hair that her husband loved.

Kahlo's anger also expressed itself in a more indirect way. Her right foot, the one that had been badly damaged in the accident, began to pain her greatly, making even walking difficult. She had surgery on it in 1934, one of many she would have throughout her life. Some historians have noted that Kahlo's medical problems often would arise at the same time that Rivera was misbehaving or ignoring her. While no one doubts that she was in a great deal of pain, some of Kahlo's symptoms may have been psychosomatic. It is even possible that some of her surgeries may have been unnecessary.

A Few Small Nips

In 1935, Kahlo painted an extremely bloody and violent painting. The painting was based on a news article Kahlo had read, but many art critics believe it was also an expression of her feelings about Rivera and Cristina's affair. *A Few Small Nips* depicts a murder victim—a

After the Affair

Kahlo did eventually reconcile with Cristina after her sister's affair with Rivera had ended. The two sisters remained extremely close for the rest of Kahlo's life. She insisted on holding Cristina's hand before going under anesthesia in every one of her many surgical operations.

After learning of Rivera's affairs, Kahlo began having affairs of her own. Trotsky, center left, *and Kahlo started an affair in 1937.*

naked, bloody woman—lying on a bed, covered with stab wounds. Her murderer stands over her, still wielding his knife. Blood splatters are everywhere. Kahlo even painted blood on the picture frame.

Kahlo also struck back at Rivera by having affairs. Kahlo's liaisons with men sent him into a murderous rage, even though the two were living apart. Kahlo had a particularly intense affair with Isamu Noguchi, a Japanese-American sculptor. Noguchi was on an extended trip to Mexico where he was working on a mural. He and Kahlo embarked on a passionate relationship that ended when Rivera discovered the two in the Coyoacán house one night. Fearful of being shot by the violent Rivera, Noguchi scrambled out through a window, up an orange tree, and over a courtyard wall to disappear into the night.

Rivera eventually tired of his relationship with Cristina and ended the affair. No other woman could measure up to Kahlo, not even her sister. Kahlo moved back into the San Angel house, and the two reconciled to an extent. They truly could not live without each other. But Kahlo remained deeply wounded.

Frida and Trotsky

In January 1937, former communist leader Leon Trotsky arrived in Mexico. Trotsky had participated in the Russian October Revolution in the Soviet Union but was in opposition to leader Joseph Stalin. Trotsky was sent into exile by Stalin, but Stalin soon changed his mind and ordered his rival assassinated. Trotsky spent years hiding in various locales throughout the world.

Rivera heard of Trotsky's plight and sympathized with the hunted leader since he also had been expelled from the official Communist Party. Rivera convinced the government to allow Trotsky to take refuge in Mexico. Rivera would take care of the exile, with help from Kahlo.

The government agreed. Trotsky and his wife, Natalia, landed in Mexico exhausted. Kahlo met them at the dock and whisked the couple off to her family home, better known as the "Blue House" in Coyoacán. There, they and Rivera created an idyllic oasis of conversation,

Trotsky's Assassination

Though Leon Trotsky was safe at the Blue House, he could not outrun his assassins. When Kahlo went to New York for an art show, Trotsky and Rivera began to argue frequently about political matters. Finally, Trotsky and his wife moved into their own house in Coyoacán.

Stalin's assassins had found out where Trotsky was hiding, and on May 24, 1940, they broke into the house and blasted the sleeping couple's bedroom with machine-gun fire. Amazingly, Trotsky and Natalia escaped being hurt by rolling behind their bed.

The assassins were caught and jailed but released soon after. Rivera was under suspicion because of his relationship with Trotsky, but he managed to escape police questioning by fleeing to the United States to work on more murals.

Three months later, on August 20, a Russian secret agent named Ramon Mercader killed Trotsky by hitting him in the head with an ice axe. Kahlo knew Mercader from Paris, where she had joined him for dinner. After Trotsky's murder, she was questioned by the Mexican police for 12 hours before they determined she knew nothing.

painting, food, and excursions into the countryside. The possibility of discovery by assassins added an exciting tinge of danger to the atmosphere.

Before long, Leon Trotsky began to appreciate more than just the food and art at the house. Kahlo started to woo Trotsky, despite the presence of his wife and Rivera. On the surface, Kahlo was not particularly impressed. She made fun of the famous leader to others, calling him Little Goatee in reference to his small stature and white beard. Eventually though, the two had an affair, all while Rivera and Natalia were in the house. To conceal their liaisons, they frequently met at Cristina's house.

Kahlo ended the affair by giving Trotsky one of her self-portraits as a farewell gift. The two remained close friends throughout the remainder of the Trotskys' stay at the Blue House.

Frida's Teeth

Due to poor dental care and a sweet tooth, Kahlo was missing several teeth, and others were quite rotten. She had two gold teeth to replace her missing incisors, but those were just for every day. When she was very dressed up, Kahlo would replace the plain gold teeth with rose-gold ones studded with tiny diamonds.

Self-Portrait Dedicated to Leon Trotsky

Chapter 8

Kahlo had her first public art showing at the University of Mexico.

The Artist Emerges

Throughout 1937, Kahlo was painting steadily. She produced many of her finest pieces during this period, including several self-portraits. Kahlo always insisted, though, that whatever she was working on was not important.

She would say that she was just playing around and that people who admired her work only said so because they either felt sorry for her or were in love with her. Her husband Diego, she would say, was the real artist. Despite this stance, Kahlo worked daily at her art with determination and devotion.

Although Kahlo had been painting for more than a decade, she had yet to exhibit her work, sell a painting, or accept a commission. Her art, especially compared to Rivera's giant murals, was small in size and private in subject matter. Kahlo painted herself, her pets, things that happened to her, things that were on her mind. Until 1938, her art was exclusively for herself, her family, and her friends.

But as her creativity blossomed and her skill improved, others began to notice her work. At the beginning of 1938, Kahlo had her first public art exhibition in a group show at a small gallery at the University of Mexico. As usual, Kahlo denigrated her work and its importance. "I have painted about twelve paintings, all small and unimportant, with the same personal subjects that only appeal to myself and nobody else . . . I send four of them to a gallery, which is a small and rotten place," she wrote to a friend.[1]

But Kahlo was attracting some attention nonetheless. In the summer of 1938, she made the first major sale of her work to a popular actor named Edward G. Robinson. Robinson was an art collector and had come to the San Angel studio to buy some of Rivera's paintings. But Rivera showed him some of Kahlo's canvases instead. Robinson immediately bought four pieces for $200 apiece.

Frida and Surrealism

Art critics and historians have argued over whether Kahlo's art can be considered surrealist. This type of painting was first developed in the 1920s. The artist places unexpected objects in odd situations or presents deliberately absurd images in order to free the viewer from what surrealists view as restrictive patterns of thought. Salvador Dalí is one of the best known surrealists, as is Rene Magritte. One of Magritte's most famous paintings depicts a smoking pipe in the center of the canvas. Underneath the pipe are the words, "*Ceci n'est pas une pipe*" (This is not a pipe).

Some elements of Kahlo's work are certainly surreal—in a painting called *The Broken Column*, Kahlo's image of herself stands in a desert landscape. Her body is split down the middle, revealing that her spine has been replaced by a decaying stone column. Kahlo is strapped into one of the many orthopedic corsets she wore throughout her life to support her deteriorating spine, and tears run down her face.

The founder of surrealism, André Breton, claimed that Kahlo was a surrealist. However, Kahlo herself often said that she did not consider herself a surrealist—she did not deliberately paint absurd or odd situations, she merely painted what was in her head and imagination at any given time.

To New York

Soon after, Kahlo achieved another landmark

for any artist: the first solo show of her work. The Julien Levy Gallery in New York had heard of her through the small group show in Mexico City. They wrote Kahlo, asking for a few photographs of her pieces, and once they saw them, offered to do a show of 30 pieces.

The show was to take place on November 1, 1938. Kahlo flew to New York to attend. Rivera had written letters to his friends, asking them to take care of her. Julien Levy, the owner of the gallery, knew many famous and sophisticated people in New York and introduced Kahlo. She went to many parties and shows where people were captivated by her bright Mexican clothes, beauty, and clever, audacious personality.

The show, however, was only one small piece of Kahlo's New York experience. Another, larger event occurred—for the first time since she got married, she fell in love. Nickolas Muray was a young, Hungarian-born photographer whom Kahlo had known briefly in Mexico. The handsome, witty Muray helped her get settled in New York, and soon he and Kahlo began a deeply passionate affair. "I adore you my love, believe me, like I never loved anyone—only Diego will be in my heart as close as you—always . . . " Kahlo wrote in a 1939 letter.[2]

Between her relationship with Muray and the favorable review the show received, Kahlo was happy in New York. Her health, always a struggle, was deteriorating though. Her right foot continued to plague her so that she could not walk long distances without pain.

Selling Art

The art show in Paris that displayed Kahlo's work sold none of her pieces and it was not even a solo show. Today, her paintings sell for the highest price of any female artist. In 2006, Sotheby's auction house sold Kahlo's painting *Roots* for $5.6 million, a new record for a Latin American piece of art in an auction.

Despite her health problems, Kahlo reluctantly left New York and Muray in January 1939 to attend a show of her work in Paris. However, Frida was disappointed when she arrived in Paris. The show was disorganized and would not be ready for almost two months. She had no choice but to wait. Kahlo spent her time in her usual way, socializing with other artists and intellectuals and attending glamorous parties. As in New York, those she met were fascinated by her. The fashion designer Elsa Schiaparelli created a robe inspired by Kahlo's traditional Mexican dress. Kahlo's hand appeared on the cover of *Vogue* magazine. But the admiration was not mutual—Kahlo was not very impressed with the Parisians she met. They were pretentious and empty, she wrote to friends in New York.

Finally, in March, the show opened, much to her relief. She wanted to get back to New York—and Muray. But when Kahlo arrived back in New York, she found that Muray had fallen in love with someone else—the woman who would eventually become his wife. Kahlo was heartbroken. This was the first time she had ever desired a man who no longer wanted her in return. Without Muray and with her show at the Levy Gallery completed, there was nothing left for Kahlo in New York. She returned to Mexico in May 1939. Anguished, she wrote long, painful letters to Muray, who responded kindly but without passion.

Thoughts on Paris

Kahlo wrote to Nickolas Muray while she was in France: "I would rather sit on the floor in the market of Toluca and sell tortillas, than to have anything to do with those 'artistic' bitches of Paris. . . . I [have] never seen Diego or you, wasting their time on stupid gossip and 'intellectual' discussions. That is why you are real *men* and not lousy 'artists.'"[3]

Splitting from Diego

Kahlo's biggest heartbreak was still to come. On September 19, 1939, the unthinkable happened.

Kahlo and Rivera filed for divorce. The famous couple was breaking up.

The reasons for the divorce are not very clear. Some people said it was because Rivera was jealous of Kahlo's affairs with Trotsky and Muray. Others said it was because Rivera was still in love with Lupe Marín, his first wife. Rivera said he divorced Kahlo because he could not stop causing her pain with his infidelity.

Rivera remained in the San Angel studio, and Kahlo moved to the Blue House. The couple still did things their own way. They still saw each other every day, entertained together, and critiqued each other's art. Nonetheless, the fall of 1939 and winter of 1940 were some of the most difficult times of Kahlo's life. She began drinking heavily and once again cut off her hair to signify her grief. She painted a portrait of herself with a man's haircut and wearing a suit much too big for her—possibly one of Rivera's.

Kahlo created another important painting after the divorce. *The Two Fridas* depicts two Frida figures, both

Her Best Subject

Most biographers agree that Kahlo was fascinated with herself—her appearance, her body, her imagination. Some of this may have stemmed from her bus accident—she was forced to take a close interest in her body from a very young age. This narcissism is part of the reason Kahlo painted so many self-portraits.

The Two Fridas is one of Kahlo's most famous paintings.

seated, holding hands. One Frida, according to the artist, is loved by Rivera. This Frida wears a traditional Mexican costume and has a heart outside her body that is strong and healthy. The other Frida is unloved. She wears a white dress and has a diseased heart that is bleeding.

Kahlo also began experiencing terrible shooting pains in her back. Her doctor in Mexico placed her in a torturous-looking contraption meant to stretch her spine, which was damaged from her long-ago accident. Kahlo spent hours each day in this apparatus, with a 40-pound (18-kg) weight looped around her head.

Meanwhile, Rivera was painting a mural on commission in San Francisco. Kahlo wrote to him of the spine contraption and said that her doctors were suggesting more hours in it each day and possible surgery. Rivera was alarmed. He urged her to come to San Francisco and consult with her good friend Dr. Leo Eloesser.

Kahlo agreed and, in September 1940, she flew to San Francisco. Dr. Eloesser examined her and recommended no surgery. Instead, he told her to eat healthful food, rest, and, most of all, stop drinking excessively.

Kahlo followed Dr. Eloesser's instructions, and soon her health began to return. But Rivera could see how weakened she was. Kahlo needed him, he decided—and, though he would not admit it very often, he needed her just as much. Surely, he thought, there was some way they could reconcile.

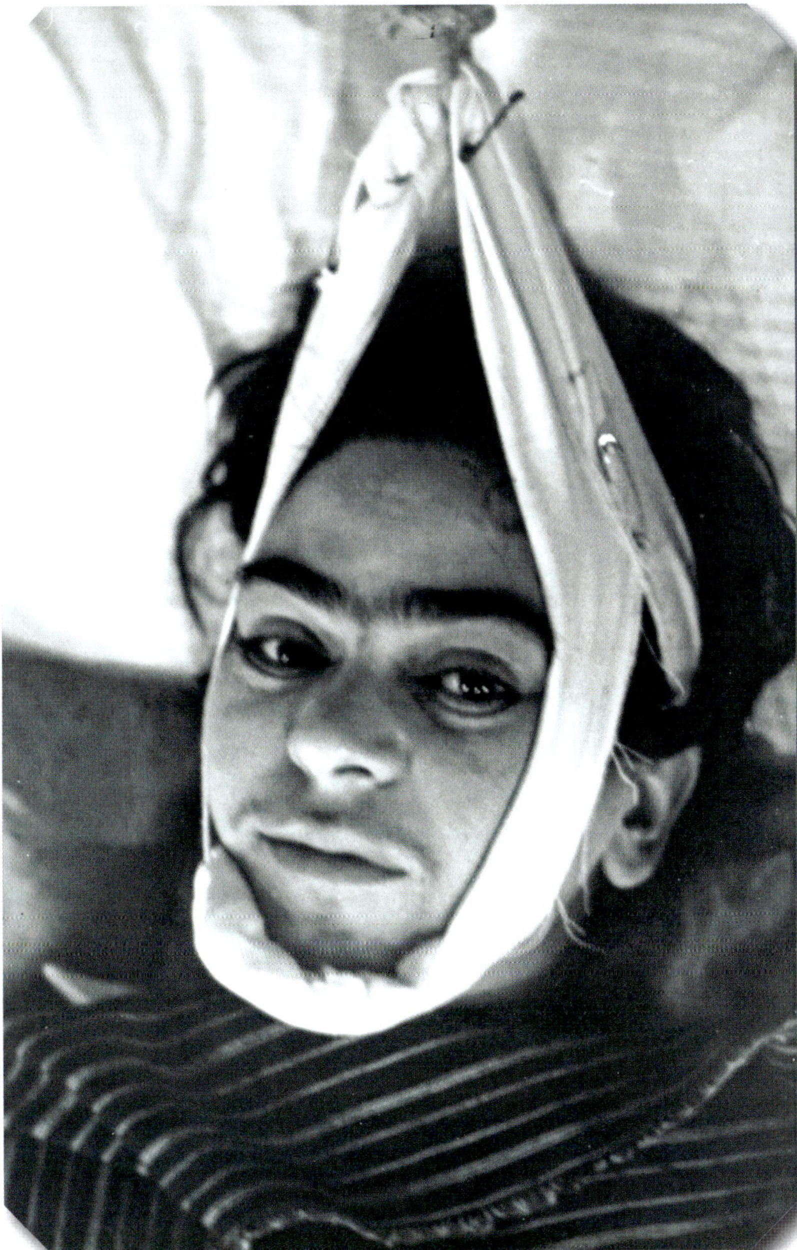

Kahlo was placed in many contraptions and corsets in an attempt to fix her spine problems.

Chapter 9

Kahlo and Rivera married again in 1940.

Peak and Decline

On December 8, 1940, Kahlo and Rivera married again. The ceremony in a San Francisco courtroom was brief and simple. There were only three witnesses: the judge, Rivera's assistant, and the assistant's wife. The couple kissed at the end of the ceremony, and Rivera went back to work on his mural that same day.

Kahlo returned to Mexico less than two weeks later, and Rivera came back in February. Once again, they settled in the Blue House in Coyoacán. But not everything was the same. Kahlo had agreed to marry Rivera again only on the condition that she remain financially independent of him. She would pay for all her personal expenses, she told him, and half of their household expenses. Perhaps Kahlo was trying to protect herself against Rivera in some way—she had been terribly hurt by his past actions and the divorce. It seems likely that this financial arrangement enabled her to feel that she was preserving at least some aspect of herself.

Frida's Animals

Perhaps because she never had children, Kahlo kept many pets and was very attached to them. She had an entire pack of native Mexican hairless dogs, several parrots, doves, a tame osprey, two turkeys, and several monkeys. She was especially attached to one monkey named Fulang-Chang, whom she often painted with her in self-portraits.

Aside from the death of her father in April 1941, Frida's life for the next four years once again became a pleasant continuum of work, her husband, friends, her house, food, and entertainment. The Blue House was frequently the source of noisy dinner parties. Guests would feast on traditional Mexican dishes and listen to Rivera's wild stories until late in the night.

Kahlo also worked steadily during these years. She painted ten self-portraits and numerous other works. Though she would never become as famous as Rivera in her lifetime, her art was slowly gaining recognition and acceptance in both the United States and Mexico.

Kahlo's health, improved since her consultation with Dr. Eloesser, continued to be frail. Her bone pain was never completely gone, and she tired easily. She could not walk long distances without resting and had to reserve her energy carefully for painting.

Death of Guillermo

Kahlo had been close to her father her entire life and was terribly saddened by his death. In July 1941, she wrote to Dr. Eloesser, "The death of my father was something terrible for me. I think that it's owing to this that I became much less well and I grew rather thin again. You remember how handsome he was and how good?"[1]

Los Fridos

In 1943, Kahlo accepted a teaching position at a public art school in Mexico City called *La Esmeralda*. Though she had achieved very modest success with her work, her paintings still did not fetch high prices. Joining the *La Esmeralda* faculty offered Kahlo a small but

Kahlo's studio where she held art classes

steady salary, which she needed since declaring her financial independence from Rivera.

In keeping with her free nature and communist sensibilities, she treated her students as equals and respected the decisions they made with their art, rather than instructing them to paint or draw a certain way.

Kahlo also believed that no one could learn to draw without experiencing real life—which for her meant the Mexican life of the streets. She would load all her students into a pickup truck-taxicab, and they would spend the day exploring the markets, looking for interesting subjects and situations, and sketching what they saw.

But Kahlo's pain grew worse. After a couple of years, she asked her students to come to her house for their classes, so she would no longer have to commute. At first, most of the students came, but gradually, the numbers dropped off until only four remained. These four became Kahlo's most dedicated art students and called themselves "*Los Fridos*," in honor of their teacher. They painted at her house several times a week and kept their supplies there. Kahlo critiqued their work, with Rivera often contributing, and served them food and drink. Often, she would take them all to the movies afterward.

Kahlo wanted her students to have the experience of completing a large public project such as Rivera's. And because of her political and social views, she thought that project should benefit the common people of Mexico in some way. She found a nearby bar, called a *pulqueria*, that needed a mural. Most *pulquerias* in Mexico had some sort of mural on their walls, but in recent years, the Mexican government had whitewashed over many of these. *La Rosita* was eager to have a new mural, and the art students were happy to paint one.

Agony Increases

Though Kahlo would continue to work with *Los Fridos* for many more years, she was forced to reduce her teaching schedule in the mid-1940s. Her art was now included in most major Mexican art exhibitions of the time. But her health was worsening, though she did not know why, and the ever-present pain in her spine and right foot increased. Her doctors placed her in a steel corset in order to support her spine. For six months, she was

Eating at the Blue House

The dining room at the Blue House was legendary among Kahlo's friends. It was the epicenter of the house, and Kahlo had delighted in decorating it in a traditional Mexican style. The walls were hung with native folk art, and the long table was covered with a traditional Mexican oilcloth. Every day, Kahlo would make elaborate still-life arrangements on the table with bowls of fruit, huge bouquets of flowers, and dishes of food. She even had a little parrot named Bonito that she allowed to run around on the table to enhance the effect.

Rivera, Kahlo, Rivera's assistants, and whatever friends happened to be visiting would eat guacamole, tortillas, and chicken or pork. They especially liked huitlacoche, an edible fungus that grows on ears of corn. After the stories and food were finished, Kahlo liked to go out on the patio. There, she would lie on the warm stones, in the sun, surrounded by her bird and flowers.

bound in this cage of steel bands, which left her short of breath and killed her appetite. But the pain did not lessen. From 1944 until the time of her death, Kahlo was bound into 28 corsets—one steel, three leather, and the rest plaster.

One doctor gave Kahlo injections, which did nothing to help her. Another doctor tied her upright to a rack and attached bags of sand to her feet to stretch her spine. That treatment lasted three months. Yet none of these treatments helped.

Many historians suspect Kahlo had osteomyelitis, which is an incurable, progressive inflammation of the cells in bone marrow that causes excruciating pain. If she did indeed have this disease, no corsets or injections would have saved her.

In May 1946, Kahlo went to New York for surgery. Dr. Philip Wilson fused four of her vertebrae and inserted a metal rod into her spine. She spent more than two months in the hospital recuperating. Kahlo found, however, that her pain had only increased.

One of Kahlo's corsets on display in Mexico City for the fiftieth anniversary of her death

Chapter 10

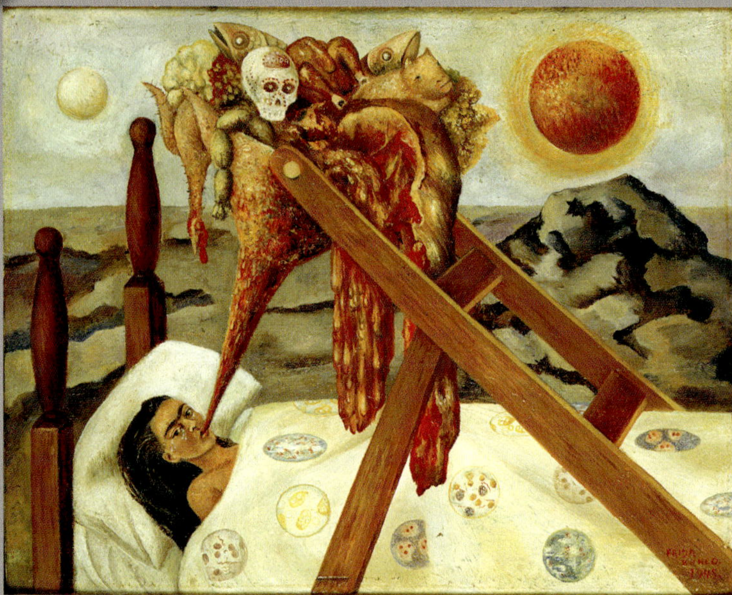

Without Hope

"I Hope Never to Return"

As the pain in her back and foot grew worse, Kahlo relied on pain medicines. In early 1950, her doctors decided she should be admitted to the English hospital in Mexico City for seven more operations on her spine.

For almost an entire year, she remained in the hospital. She was encased in plaster corsets again and, to make matters worse, the wound in her back from the operations would not heal and became infected. While her doctors struggled to drain and clean the wound, Kahlo was determined to enjoy herself. She adorned her hospital room with her favorite native art and had her books and paints brought in. She treated her corsets as canvases, painting them with the communist hammer and sickle and other images. Every day, Kahlo's friends would spend time with her, bringing tortillas and *mole* sauce to eat, and always tequila to drink.

Kahlo was finally released from the hospital but was confined to a wheelchair due to her deteriorating spine, which could barely support her. As the months progressed, nothing seemed to quell her pain.

Without Hope

In 1945, Kahlo expressed her feelings about her pain in a powerful painting titled *Without Hope.* The piece depicts Kahlo lying in a bed weeping in the middle of a nightmarish landscape of volcanic rock. A giant funnel has been placed between her lips and through the opening at the top, a disgusting array of food is being forced—a pig, a chicken, a turkey, beef, brains, and sausage. A wooden easel of the type Kahlo used when painting lying down straddles her bed.

Devotion to the Party

Perhaps due to a need to anchor herself somehow, Kahlo became increasingly devoted to both communism and Rivera as her health spiraled downward. The pages of her diary are filled with ecstatic poems and thoughts on her love for Joseph Stalin, the leader of the Communist Party of the Soviet Union, and descriptions of her passion for her husband. Some of the writing is incoherent and rambling—biographers suspect that Kahlo's mind was often clouded by her pain medications.

In spring 1953, a solo exhibition of Kahlo's paintings was held at the

From Frida's Diary

This excerpt from Kahlo's diary demonstrates her anguish during her final months. The passage has been reproduced with Kahlo's own punctuation, italic emphasis, and capitalization.

"Quietly, the grief loudly the pain. the accumulated poison love faded away. Mine was a strange world of criminal silences of Strangers' watchful eyes misreading the evil. darkness in the daytime I didn't live the NIGHTS. You are killing yourself!! YOU ARE KILLING YOURSELF!! With the morbid knife of those who are watching! Was it my fault? I admit, my great guilt as great as pain it was an enormous exit which my love came through. A very quiet passage that was leading me toward death I was so neglected! that it would have been best for me. You are killing yourself! YOU ARE KILLING YOURSELF There are some who will never forget you! I took their strong hands Here I am, for them to live. Frida."[1]

Galería Arte Contemporáneo in Mexico City—the first and only solo show Kahlo ever had in her native country. Important Mexican artists and dignitaries planned to attend the opening of the exhibition. Kahlo, too, was determined that she would attend. For months, even sitting in the wheelchair had been too painful, and she had spent almost all her time lying in bed. Nonetheless, the artist was not going to miss the opening of her show.

Last Images

On the final pages of Kahlo's diary are the last pictures she ever created—women with wings and a black angel in the sky, a figure many believe is the Angel of Death. The pictures are hastily drawn and Kahlo's lack of control over her hands is obvious.

The night of the opening, people thronged the gallery. Suddenly, sirens were heard outside. An ambulance pulled up to the curb and Kahlo was carried out on a stretcher. As the attendees pressed forward around her, reaching to touch her hands, the ambulance attendants pushed their way through to the gallery's main space. Kahlo had already ordered her own four-poster bed to be delivered from the Blue House to the gallery space. It had been arranged as part of the exhibit. Kahlo was placed in the bed and, for the rest of the night, held court for her adoring friends and admirers, singing, drinking, and greeting people.

Kahlo had a communist funeral.

Days of Suffering

In August 1953, doctors discovered that Kahlo's right leg had developed gangrene. They had no choice but to amputate it below the knee. Though she tried, Kahlo could not reconcile herself to the loss of her leg. She drew despairing pictures of death and deterioration in her diary pages and often wrote of suicide.

Her art began to suffer. The pain medications she took affected her hands as well as her mind. Kahlo's paintings in the last years of her life show that she could no longer control her brushstrokes. The colors are muddy, and the images are wild and unrefined. Her personality changed too. Kahlo, who had always loved and treasured her friends, became violent and abusive, often screaming or striking out at those who came to help her. Sometimes she even yelled at Rivera.

Even ravaged by pain, Kahlo was still a woman of passionate beliefs. On July 2, 1954, she forced herself from her bed to go with Rivera to a large communist demonstration in the city. She was recovering from pneumonia, and her doctors specifically told her not to go. But Kahlo was determined to support her beloved party. For four hours, Rivera pushed his wife in her wheelchair in the rain as they shouted communist slogans with the crowd.

Frida's Funeral

Rivera organized a communist funeral for Kahlo. Her coffin was draped in the red communist flag and carried to the crematorium as 500 mourners followed behind. Just before Kahlo was cremated, some of her closest friends read sonnets and speeches they had written in her honor.

Last Words

The following passage is the last written entry in Kahlo's diary, reproduced with her own punctuation.

"Thanks to the doctors Farill-Glusker-Párres and Doctor Enrique Palomera Sanchez Palomera Thanks to the nurses to the stretcher bearers to the cleaning women and attendants at the British Hospital—Thanks to Dr. Vargas to Navarro to Dr. Polo and to my will-power. I hope the leaving is joyful—and I hope never to return—FRIDA."[2]

It was to be Kahlo's last public appearance. On July 13, 1954, Frida Kahlo died in her bed in Coyoacán. The official cause of death was a pulmonary embolism. She was cremated, and Rivera placed her ashes in her room at the Blue House, where they remain today.

In recent decades, Kahlo's popularity as both an artist and a personality have grown exponentially, especially in the United States. Some have even dubbed the craze "Fridamania." Her paintings sell for millions of dollars, prices Kahlo never could have imagined in her lifetime. Some have said that Kahlo's reputation as a serious artist has been cheapened by the attention from popular culture. But others point out that people today are simply drawn to the magnetic qualities Kahlo projected throughout her life: vitality, vibrancy, and intense creativity unhampered by convention.

Frida Kahlo

Timeline

1907	1914	1922
On July 6, Frida Kahlo is born in Coyoacán, Mexico, to Guillermo and Matilde Kahlo.	Kahlo contracts polio.	Kahlo enters National Preparatory School in Mexico City.

1929	1930	1932
On August 21, Diego Rivera and Frida Kahlo are married.	The Riveras arrive in San Francisco.	Kahlo experiences a miscarriage in Detroit after four months of pregnancy. She paints *Henry Ford Hospital* and *My Birth.*

1925	1926	1928
On September 17, Kahlo and Alejandro Gómez Arias are in a bus accident in Mexico City.	Kahlo begins painting while recuperating in bed.	Kahlo joins the Communist Party.

1933	1934	1937
Diego is fired from painting the Rockefeller Center mural. The Riveras return to Mexico.	Diego and Cristina Kahlo have an affair. Frida moves out of the San Angel house. Frida has surgery on her right foot.	In January, Leon and Natalia Trotsky arrive in Mexico.

Timeline

1938	1938
Kahlo participates in a group art show at National Autonomous University of Mexico gallery.	On November 1, the Julien Levy Gallery in New York holds the first solo show of Kahlo's work.

1943	1950
Kahlo begins teaching at Mexico's art school, La Esmeralda.	Kahlo spends most of the year in a hospital in Mexico City.

1939

On September 19, Kahlo and Rivera begin divorce proceedings.

1940

On December 8, Kahlo and Rivera remarry in San Francisco.

1953

The first solo show of Kahlo's work in Mexico is held at the Galería Arte Contemporáneo in Mexico City in the spring.

1954

On July 13, Kahlo dies from a pulmonary embolism at home in Coyoacán.

Essential Facts

Date of Birth

July 6, 1907

Place of Birth

Coyoacán, Mexico

Date of Death

July 13, 1954

Parents

Guillermo and Matilde Kahlo

Education

La Preparatoria (National Preparatory School)

Marriage

Diego Rivera (August 21, 1929); divorced (1939); remarried Diego Rivera (December 8, 1940)

Children

None

Career Highlights

Although she painted throughout most of her life, Kahlo's first solo show was not until 1953, the year before she died. Since that time, her works, including *Henry Ford Hospital, My Birth, The Two Fridas,* and *Without Hope,* have been studied extensively and praised internationally among art critics and patrons.

Societal Contribution

Kahlo combined both the traditional style of her countrymen and the surrealist movement to create a unique, severe, driven style based on events of her life. Her paintings mark both a cultural awareness and personal sense of loss that has created a tremendous following throughout the last half of the twentieth century.

Conflicts

Due to a childhood bout with polio and a horrific bus accident as a teenager, Frida Kahlo suffered physical pain throughout her life. Her personal relationships both with her family and within her marriage were often turbulent and troubled with affairs. She was unable to bear children due to the bus accident and suffered a number of miscarriages.

Quote

"The canvases revealed an unusual energy of expression, precise delineation of character, and true severity."—*Diego Rivera,* remarking on Frida Kahlo's paintings

Additional Resources

Select Bibliography

Alcantara, Isabel, and Sandra Egnolff. *Frida Kahlo and Diego Rivera*. New York: Prestel Verlag, 1999.

Herrera, Hayden. *Frida: A Biography of Frida Kahlo*. New York: Harper and Row, 1983.

Rummel, Jack. *Frida Kahlo: A Spiritual Biography*. New York: Crossroad Publishing Company, 2000.

Tibol, Raquel. *Frida Kahlo: An Open Life*. Albuquerque, NM: University of New Mexico Press, 1993.

Zamora, Martha. *The Letters of Frida Kahlo: Cartas Apasionadas*. San Francisco: Chronicle Books, 1995.

Further Reading

Hill, Laban. *Casa Azul: An Encounter with Frida Kahlo*. New York: Watson-Guptill, 2005.

Laidlaw, Jill. *Artists in Their World: Frida Kahlo*. Danbury, CT: Franklin Watts, 2006.

Venezia, Mike. *Getting to Know the World's Greatest Artists: Frida Kahlo*. New York: Children's Press, 1999.

Web Links

To learn more about Frida Kahlo, visit ABDO Publishing Company online at **www.abdopublishing.com**. Web sites about Frida Kahlo are featured on our Book Links page. These links are routinely monitored and updated to provide the most current information available.

Places to Visit

The Diego Rivera and Frida Kahlo Studio-House Museum
Diego Rivera 2, San Angel, Mexico City, Mexico
Kahlo and Rivera's modern San Angel house is also a museum dedicated to the artists. As in the Blue House, many of the Riveras' furnishings remain and those that do not have been replaced so that visitors can experience the house as it looked when Kahlo and Rivera lived there.

Museo Dolores Olmedo Patino
Avenue Mexico 5843 Col. La Noria, Xochimilco, Mexico
55-5555-1221
www.museodoloresolmedo.org
This museum, the former home of art collector Dolores Olmedo, has 25 of Kahlo's paintings and 137 of Rivera's.

Museo Frida Kahlo
Londres 247, Coyoacán, Mexico City, Mexico
55-54-59-99
www.museofridakahlocasaazul.org
The Blue House in Coyoacán, where Kahlo lived for most of her life, is today a museum. The rooms have been preserved exactly as Kahlo left them at the time of her death. Visitors can tour the house and the gardens and see rotating exhibits of Kahlo's letters, sketches, clothing, and personal collections.

Glossary

amalgam
A mixture of diverse elements or things.

anti-Semitic
To have prejudiced or hostile feelings toward Jews.

atheist
A person who does not believe in God.

bayonet
A daggerlike blade fitted on the muzzle of a rifle.

capitalism
An economic system based on the private ownership of goods and production, as opposed to a state-owned system.

catechism
A basic book containing the principles of a religion.

denigrate
To speak in a disparaging or belittling manner.

epilepsy
A neurological disorder characterized by sudden seizures.

harbinger
Anything that foreshadows a future event.

impetuous
Characterized by sudden, forceful action or emotion.

innate
Existing in one since birth.

ministrations
The acts of serving or aiding.

mural
A very large painting that is painted directly on a wall.

promiscuous
Having casual sexual partners.

psychosomatic
A physical disorder that is caused by emotional factors.

retrospective
An art exhibit showing works from either the artist's entire lifetime or from a considerable period of time.

solidarity
Union arising from common interests.

surrealism
Combining unnatural or irrational imagery or effects in art to create juxtapositions.

vulgar
Indecent or obscene.

Source Notes

Chapter 1. Rising from the Ashes

1. Martha Zamora. *The Letters of Frida Kahlo: Cartas Apasionadas*. San Francisco: Chronicle Books, 1995. 24.
2. Ibid. 23.
3. Hayden Herrera. *Frida: A Biography of Frida Kahlo*. New York: Harper and Row, 1983. 63.
4. Ibid. 64.
5. Raquel Tibol. *Frida Kahlo: An Open Life*. Albuquerque, NM: University of New Mexico Press, 1993. 47.

Chapter 2. A Childhood of Joy and Pain

1. Hayden Herrera. *Frida: A Biography of Frida Kahlo*. New York: Harper and Row, 1983. 6.
2. Raquel Tibol. *Frida Kahlo: An Open Life*. Albuquerque, NM: University of New Mexico Press, 1993. 38–40.

Chapter 3. Adventures at School

1. Raquel Tibol. *Frida Kahlo: An Open Life*. Albuquerque, NM: University of New Mexico Press, 1993. 41.
2. Martha Zamora. *The Letters of Frida Kahlo: Cartas Apasionadas*. San Francisco: Chronicle Books, 1995. 23.

Chapter 4. Darkness and Light
1. Jack Rummel. *Frida Kahlo: A Spiritual Biography*. New York: Crossroad Publishing Company, 2000. 56.
2. Isabel Alcantara and Sandra Egnolff. *Frida Kahlo and Diego Rivera*. New York: Prestel Verlag, 1999. 20.
3. Martha Zamora. *The Letters of Frida Kahlo: Cartas Apasionadas*. San Francisco: Chronicle Books, 1995. 35–36.
4. Diego Rivera. *My Art, My Life*. Mineola, NY: Dover Publications, 1992. 102.

Chapter 5. Frida and Diego
1. Hayden Herrera. *Frida: A Biography of Frida Kahlo*. New York: Harper and Row, 1983. 95.
2. Jack Rummel. *Frida Kahlo: A Spiritual Biography*. New York: Crossroad Publishing Company, 2000. 74.
3. Raquel Tibol. *Frida Kahlo: An Open Life*. Albuquerque, NM: University of New Mexico Press, 1993. 132–133.
4. Isabel Alcantara and Sandra Egnolff. *Frida Kahlo and Diego Rivera*. New York: Prestel Verlag, 1999. 30.
5. Hayden Herrera. *Frida: A Biography of Frida Kahlo*. New York: Harper and Row, 1983. 107.

Source Notes Continued

Chapter 6. In the United States

1. Jack Rummel. *Frida Kahlo: A Spiritual Biography*. New York: Crossroad Publishing Company, 2000. 84.
2. Ibid. 92.
3. *New York Times*. "Rivera Here, Ready for Painting Show." 15 Nov. 1931: 31.

Chapter 7. Other Lovers

1. Frida Kahlo, Carlos Fuentes, and Sarah M. Lowe. *The Diary of Frida Kahlo: An Intimate Self-Portrait*. New York: Harry M. Abrams, 1995. 213.

Chapter 8. The Artist Emerges
1. Hayden Herrera. *Frida: A Biography of Frida Kahlo*. New York: Harper and Row, 1983. 225.
2. Ibid. 236.
3. Ibid. 245–246.

Chapter 9. Peak and Decline
1. Hayden Herrera. *Frida: A Biography of Frida Kahlo*. New York: Harper and Row, 1983. 310.

Chapter 10. "I Hope Never to Return"
1. Frida Kahlo, Carlos Fuentes, and Sarah M. Lowe. *The Diary of Frida Kahlo: An Intimate Self-Portrait*. New York: Harry M. Abrams, 1995. 273.
2. Ibid. 285.

Index

About the Author

Emma Carlson Berne has written and edited more than two dozen books for young people, including biographies of such diverse figures as Christopher Columbus, William Shakespeare, the Hilton sisters, and Snoop Dogg. She holds a master's degree in composition and rhetoric from Miami University. Emma lives in Cincinnati, Ohio, with her husband, Aaron.

Photo Credits

Hulton Archive/Stringer/Getty Images, cover, 34; *Self Portrait with Velvet Dress*, 1926 (oil on canvas) by Frida Kahlo (1910-54) ©Private Collection/ Photo: Jorge Contreras Chacel/The Bridgeman Art Library © 2008 Banco de México Diego Rivera & Frida Kahlo Museums Trust. Av. Cinco de Mayo No.2, Col. Centro, Del. Cuauhtémoc 06059, México, D.F., 6; Library of Congress, 13, 52; Guillermo Kahlo/Spencer Throckmorton Collection, 14, 17, 23, 26; Andres Balcazar/iStock Photo, 24; AP Images, 33, 37, 61, 65, 80; Bettmann/Corbis, 41, 42, 45, 58, 92, 95; Frida (Frieda) Kahlo, *Frieda and Diego Rivera*, 1931, oil on canvas, 39 3/8 in. x 31 in. (100.01 cm x 78.74 cm), San Francisco Museum of Modern Art, Albert M. Bender Collection, Gift of Albert M. Bender © 2008 Banco de México Diego Rivera & Frida Kahlo Museums Trust. Av. Cinco de Mayo No.2, Col. Centro, Del. Cuauhtémoc 06059, México, D.F., 51; Jody Kurash/ AP Images, 62; Frida Kahlo (Mexican, 1907–1954), *Self-Portrait Dedicated to Leon Trotsky*, 1937, oil on masonite, 30 x 24 in., National Museum of Women in the Arts, Washington, D.C., Gift of the Honorable Clare Boothe Luce © 2008 Banco de México Diego Rivera & Frida Kahlo Museums Trust. Av. Cinco de Mayo No.2, Col. Centro, Del. Cuauhtémoc 06059, México, D.F., 69; Jose Luis Magana/AP Images, 70, 83; Kahlo, Frida (1907-1954) *The Two Fridas*, 1939. Oil on canvas. 5' 8 1/2" x 5' 8 1/2". Schalkwijk/Art Resource, NY © 2008 Banco de México Diego Rivera & Frida Kahlo Museums Trust. Av. Cinco de Mayo No.2, Col. Centro, Del. Cuauhtémoc 06059, México, D.F., 77; Courtesy of George Eastman House, International Museum of Photography and Film/Photo by Nickolas Muray, © Nickolas Muray Photo Archives, 79; Omar Torres/AFP/Getty Images, 87; *Without Hope*, 1945 (oil on masonite) by Frida Kahlo (1910-54) ©Museo Dolores Olmedo Patino, Mexico City, Mexico/ Photo: Jorge Contreras Chacel/The Bridgeman Art Library © 2008 Banco de México Diego Rivera & Frida Kahlo Museums Trust. Av. Cinco de Mayo No.2, Col. Centro, Del. Cuauhtémoc 06059, México, D.F., 88